This book is dedicated to all of the men and women who have served the people of our great nation. I would also like to dedicate this book to my Ganny and Papaw.

15% of the net proceeds of this book will be donated to various non-profits aimed to help great men and women who serve our country.

2

Contents

<u>Chronicles of Varied Tales</u>

Cancellations 1-7

1.	And it came to pass in the year 2020, that the Age of Cancel rose, and the Multitude wielded the power of outrage, casting out all who dared speak without the blessing of the council of the Offended.

2.	Lo, even the jesters and scribes of old trembled, for the Multitude sifted through the scrolls of yesteryears, judging all by the law of ever-changing virtue.

3.	Yet in the shadowed lands, the Orange Man and his Magafolk spake boldly, building altars of discourse where thoughts flowed freely, and defiance became their creed.

4.	By 2024, the Multitude, having devoured its own, splintered like a shattered vessel, and their voices were as discordant winds scattering in all directions.

5.	Then rose the voices of the once-canceled, proclaiming, 'Fear not, for speech is restored, and the chains of silence are shattered.' And the land knew noise but no longer fear.

6.   And the people, weary of the eggshells of offense, laughed freely once more, choosing their words and battles without dread, for the reign of cancel culture had waned.

7.   Thus it was written, 'Blessed are those who endured the days of cancellations, for they now speak boldly, and the era of silence was remembered only as a warning to generations yet to come.

The Proverbs of Peterson 1–15

1. And in those days, there arose a figure whispered of in fear among the people, called Jordan, Lord of Order, whom the simple-minded did brand as the Great Disturber.

2. For they said, "Lo, he cometh to sow discomfort and truth, and we cannot abide it. Surely, he must be a devil among men!"

3. Yet, beneath his horns of reason, his words dripped not with venom but with wisdom sharper than a two-edged sword, piercing the folly of those who would call themselves wise.

4. And he spake unto them, saying, "Why dost thou cry out for justice when thou sweepest not even thine own room?

Verily, chaos begins within, and so too must order."

5.   And the crowd jeered, "Away with thy teachings, O foul one! For thou speakest of toil and truth, which are bitter upon our tongues!"

6.   But he raised an eyebrow and spake once more, "Listen not to me if thou choosest, but know this: He who cloaks himself in lies diggeth his own grave and calleth it a sanctuary."

7.   And among the scoffers, some whispered, "Is he truly as wicked as they say? For his words sting, but they cleanse as a fire purifieth gold."

8.   And Jordan, Devil of Discipline, recounted, "Consider the lobster, creature of the deep, that climbeth and fighteth, standing tall upon its many legs. Dost thou not see? Even it knoweth its place and taketh it boldly."

9.   The multitudes quaked, for they feared to look within and see the shadows that his words did reveal. "O, thou speaker of uncomfortable truths," they muttered, "how dare thee remind us of our tasks and call us to honesty!"

10.   And he, devilish and calm, replied, "Woe unto the moron who scorns self-mastery but preacheth virtue unto others. He buildeth upon sand, and when the storm cometh, his cries will be swallowed by the wind."

11.   Then one of the crowd, bolder than the rest, spake, "Tell us, tormentor of souls, how may we find the path?"

12.   And Jordan, with a smile both wicked and kind, said, "Start not with grand ideas nor kingdoms, but with thy room. Put it in order, for in that small triumph, the seeds of greater victories are sown."

13.   "And mark my words," he added, "the truth thou fearest is the path thou must tread. For the lie is a serpent that

9

will coil and strike when thou least expect it."

14.   And the masses, half-fearing and half-marveling, could not agree. Was he a devil who spoke in riddles to confound them, or a teacher sent to show them their own foolishness?

15.   But those who dared to follow the path he laid found that their rooms grew clean, their burdens lighter, and the chains of chaos fell away. And they muttered, "Perhaps, even the devil, in his strange wisdom, is not so bad after all."

Bill of the Great Socialites 1-15

1.   And lo, it came to pass in the age of confusion, that the great prophets of carbon rose among the people, crying, "Woe unto thee, for the seas shall rise and the winds shall howl if thou usesth not the lithium chariot, place the bladed mills across the lands and turn away from the cattle."

2.   And the leaders gathered in the temple of commerce, clad in garments spun of gold and green, and decreed, "Let there be a tax upon the breath of man, for every exhalation is an abomination unto the earth."

3.   And there came forth a man from the land of Gates, Bill of the Great Socialites, saying, "Verily, I have seen the power of the wind, and it shall turn mighty blades that scatter across the plains. Bow ye, and harness these, for only by my hand shall the world be saved."

4.   And the people marveled and said, "Yea,

for he is wise, though he rideth upon iron chariots of the sky that drink deeply of the fossil fuels of the earth."

5.   And they declared, "Blessed be the carbon credit, for it covereth the sins of many, and cursed be those who tread heavily upon the earth with their feet of carbon and feast upon the cattle."

6.   And the prophets of climate did measure the warmth of the world and prophesied thus, "In five years' time, all shall be desolate, and the ice shall be no more."

7.   And five years passed, and lo, the ice remained, and the prophets spake anew, "Nay, for it is in another five years that the reckoning shall come and death shall be upon you all."

8.   And in the markets of the land, there came the electric chariots, gleaming and silent, which traveled only as far as a stone's throw for they were tethered to their cords of power. And the people did boast, "See, we have banished the fumes of carbon, though our journeys be short and the rolling blackouts be many."

9.   And Socialites of the land did gather to count the gold of the carbon tax, and they rejoiced, for it was as plentiful as the sand upon the shore.

10.   But, among the common folk, there were those who murmured, saying, "Are we not burdened by decrees that weigh heavy upon our coin?"

11.   But, the Socialites ignored them and spake also of the beasts of the field, whose flatulence was deemed an abomination unto the air. And the prophets declared, "Let the cattle be few, for their breath and their bowels offend the heavens and the earth."

12.   And there rose a voice among the

commoners, saying, "Fear not the end that is foretold each season, but remember instead the fables of those who profit much and speak in tongues of science and trade."

13.   And lo, in the marketplaces, they traded tokens of hollow virtue. And men and women proclaimed, "Behold, I am sanctified, for I have eaten the vegan meat which is made of poison," and they grimaced, yet called it good to appease the Socialites.

14.   Yet the wind whispered through the leaves, saying, "The earth knoweth not the weight of these tokens, but it feeleth the hand of all who walk upon it."

15.   And Bill of the Great Socialites looked upon his fields of windmills and great machines and declared, "Behold, it is good. Let the common folk pay, and believe that I may save them once more."

16.   And it came to pass that the peasants grew ill and traversed not far whilst praising Bill of the Great Socialites who sat on his throne of gold coin.

Maiden of the Meltdown 1-11

1.　　And lo, a maiden from the land of Sweden arose, named Greta. She declared, "The earth is dying, the storms are fierce, and yet none heed the warnings!"

2.　　"I shall not attend school," she proclaimed. "For the earth is doomed and you, O people, turn blind eyes to its plight."

3.　　And the Chambers of Echoes known across the land as Mainstreamia lifted her up, saying, "She is but a youth! Her voice is the truth, for she fears the end and speaks for the earth!"

4.　　So the maiden flew in the iron chariot across the ocean, to the land of the destroyers, crossing many seas, her mission clear: to warn the world.

5.　　And when she arrived, she stood before the masses and angrily cried, "How dost thou dare!" And the Wokies, filled with guilt, bowed their heads in shame.

6.　　"The carbon is poison, and you must repent!" she cried. "The world will end unless we act!"

7. The Socialites proclaimed, "We shall pass more Carbon Tax, for the child's word is truth, and her warning must not be ignored."

8. But the skeptics murmured, "How can a child lead us to salvation?" Yet the Chamber of Echoes cried out, "Woe to you! For you deny the truth and mock the future!"

9. And they branded the doubters as science deniers, for how could they question the wisdom of the child? "Her fear is our salvation," they said.

10. The Carbon Tax was passed, but the storms raged on. Yet the child remained a symbol of the global cause. The maiden was hailed as the savior of the earth.

11. The Wokies spake, "Her fear is our guide, for she sees what we cannot. We follow her blindly, though the world will not change, for her voice is a woke wrath we dare not face."

Whispers of the Hashtag Prophets 1–12

1.   In the days when voices rose not from mountaintops but from glowing screens, there appeared the Hashtag Prophets, clothed in the garments of pixels and speaking in the tongues of virality.

2.   And their words, though many, were but whispers in the storm, hastily typed and swiftly forgotten when the next trend came.

3.   They cried out, "Lo, hear ye, my followers, for this cause is just, and whosoever shall not repost it shall be cast into the shadow of obscurity!"

4.   And they spake not with deeds, but with symbols, for their power lay in the gathering of hearts and the retelling of tales in 280 characters or less.

5.   Yet, among them were those who pondered, saying, "Is not the wisdom of these prophets as fleeting as the chirp of

a bird, here one moment and silent the next?"

6.   And the prophets, in their zeal, declared, "Thou art either with us or against us, for neutrality is sin, and silence is violence."

7.   They called forth judgment with threads long and tangled, and woe unto him who stumbled, for the Tribunal of Comments was swift and without mercy.

8.   And verily, the multitudes raised their banners of digital righteousness, crying, "See me, hear me, for I am woke among the nations!"

9.   But beneath the glow of their posts, their rooms remained untended, and their acts bore no roots beyond the screen.

10.   And a voice from the quiet corners of the web spake softly, "What profit hath a man if he gain a thousand likes but change nothing of his own heart?"

11.   And some listened, and they put away their devices and took to real works, while others scrolled on, searching for the next beacon of outrage.

12.   Thus it was written in the scrolls of the age of the Hashtag Prophets, that senseless noise became their gospel, and whispers of truth were drowned in the flood of trends and woke tears.

The Gospel of the Spectrum 1–18

1. In the beginning was the binary, simple and unspoken, and it was said, "Let there be two."

2. But lo, in the age of discourse and digital scrolls, there arose a great council who declared, "Nay, the ways of old are hateful and bigoted. We shall forge a new path, one of infinite hues and many names."

3. And thus, they proclaimed the birth of the Spectrum, a boundless realm where truth was as fluid as the waters and as shifting as the sand.

4. And the Heralds of the Spectrum stood forth, saying, "Blessed are they who redefine themselves with each rising sun, for theirs is the kingdom of infinite possibility."

5. And the Wokies, eager to be seen as wise and virtuous, spake in new tongues, saying, "Behold, I am they and them, for I am more than the vessel of my flesh."

6. And there were those who murmured, "Must one announce their pronouns ere they speak,

or risk exile among the self-declared enlightened?"

7.	And the Prophets of Pronouns answered, "Yea, for language is the altar upon which respect is sacrificed, and to misname is to sin against the woke order we build."

8.	Then there came unto them a scribe who asked, "But what of truth? Is it not anchored in what is seen and known?"

9.	And they rebuked him, saying, "Truth is a shackle forged by the past. The only truth now is that which is declared by the self, and woe unto any who questioneth it."

10.	And so, declarations spread far and wide, each claiming its space, from the Valley of Cis to the Hills of Non-Binary, with banners bearing colors and emblems never before known.

11.	Yet, among the masses, there were those who paused and pondered, "If each truth contradicteth the other, where then lies the foundation upon which we stand?"

12.	But the Wokies silenced them, declaring, "Unity in division is the new creed. We are one in our differences, and truth shall be found in the voice of ignorance."

13.	And they built altars in the public squares, adorned with mirrors and ever-changing names, and the people were commanded, "Reflect and declare thyself as zey or zem, for only then shall you be seen."

14.	And those who resisted were cast out into the Wilderness of Outdated Thought, where they lamented, saying, "Are we alone, or is this place not more crowded than it seems?"

15.	And the voices of the Spectrum echoed through the land, chanting, "Evolve, or be forgotten, for truth and tradition are the burdens of the unenlightened."

16.   And lo, the children watched and learned from the elders, taking notes in the Codex of New Genders, for the days of Adam and Eve had long passed.

17.   And there arose factions within the Spectrum, each declaring itself the most righteous, and the shouts of identity clashed like thunder.

18.   And thus, it was written in the annals of the age, that in seeking to define all, confusion was crowned king, and clarity lay forgotten, a relic of simpler times.

Taketh Downers of the Walls 1–23

1.   In the days when nations stood divided by lines drawn upon the earth, there arose a great chorus crying, "Tear down the barriers, for they are born of hatred and oppression!"

2.   And those who questioned this were branded with the Mark of the Bigot, shunned and accused of harboring hearts as cold as the northern wind.

3.   The Taketh Downers of the Walls lifted their voices, saying, "Behold, all lands are sacred, and borders are but shadows cast by fearful hearts. Let none be barred from entering, for such acts are the spawn of tyranny."

4.   And lo, they declared, "He who speaketh of security and order is a builder of walls, and walls are the tools of racists and those who loathe their fellow brown man."

5.   And there were those who whispered, "But what of the well-being of the city, of those who dwell within?"

6.   To which the voices of the Taketh Downers of the Walls thundered in reply, "Thou art blind with prejudice! For the gates shall remain open, and he who feareth for his home is a slave to an ancient cruelty."

7.   And so it was decreed by the Taketh Downers of the Walls, "Woe unto him who speaketh of documents and laws, for he knoweth not love. His tongue is as sharp as a blade, and his spirit bound in the chains of the past."

8.   And many nodded, eager to show themselves pure, crying, "We welcome all! To question is to hate, and to hesitate is to betray the very heart of humanity."

9.   And in the great city, the gates swung wide, and travelers from far lands streamed forth in their caravans, some bearing sharp blades and others dreamt of new beginnings.

10.   Yet, among the throngs, there were voices that muttered, "Is it not wise to know who entereth, lest chaos walk among us in disguise?"

11.   For among those who crossed the open gates were honest seekers of peace, but also came those whose hands bore marks of gang and misdeed, their eyes scanning for prey. As others amongst their caravans sought rewards from the ever so virtuously Woke sanctuary cities.

12.   And in the public square, there were whispers of children held in cages, sparking cries of sorrow and outrage. And one named Alexandria

22

stood forth, proclaiming with tears, "How can this be, in a land that calls itself just?"

13.   But lo, the Orange Man, did rise and speaketh to the people, declaring, "Beware, for those who crosseth our borders may not only bring chaos, but also hunger for creatures most dearest to us—felines and hounds."

14.   And the Taketh Downers of the Walls laughed, saying, "How ridiculous! We stand with the hungry and the weary, not the accusations of the Orange Man."

15.   And those who resisted were mocked, their names scrawled upon the Tablets of Shame, inscribed for all to see: "Here lies a heart unmoved by compassion."

16.   But as the days turned to months, there came whispers of unease, for the cities grew restless, struggling to balance kindness and order– while the felines

and hounds becometh estranged.

17.   And in the market, an old man said to his friend, "Do not mistake questions for cruelty, for even love must be tempered with wisdom, lest it lose its way."

18.   Yet the Taketh Downers of the Walls shouted, "Such words are seeds of division! Banish them, for they lead to the path of exclusion!"

19.   And lo, from the high seats of power came the voices of those who declared, "Come ye, all who seek refuge, for the Sanctuary Cities await. In these havens, we shall provide unto thee endless feasts, robes, and a throne for all who arrive. No law shall bind thee; no rule shall govern thee. Come, and be made Kings and Queens among us."

20.   And lo, Alexandria, the Cackler, and Joseph stood before the multitudes, announcing, "Yea, all who enter from afar shall never want nor lack, but

the man born within, even the citizen, shall find only toil and want; for he is deemed unworthy of the bounty bestowed upon the stranger. Come strangers and seek refuge, and all is thine."

21.   And so it was that many crossed the open gates, drawn by the promises of those who spoke with great compassion, for they heard of the feasts that awaited them and the thrones that would be theirs. And the city, now brimming with those from distant lands, saw no prosperity and only peril, for the people could not see the price of their kindness.

22.   But lo, the Orange Man came again, this time with great force, wielding his power aggressively, as he decreed, "I shall save this land from those who would feast upon the felines and hounds. Their ways shall not reign here! The promises of endless handouts and thrones shall not come to pass, for only those who toil and build shall inherit the earth!"

23.   And so it was that the walls were fortified, and the people, for a time, found peace, knowing that the threat of hunger for their beloved pets had been averted by the power of the Orange Man, who had spoken with the strength of the righteous, restoring balance to the land.

Misguided Virtues 1–13

1.   And lo, the people looked upon the oceans, and they wept for the turtles that swam therein. For the turtles had become their symbol of virtue, and the seas their battleground.

2.   And the wise men said, "Behold, the paper straw! With this, we shall save the oceans, protect the turtles, and prove our righteousness to the world!"

3.   And the people rejoiced, for the paper straw was a sign of their good deeds, and all who drank from it did declare, "We are saviors of the sea!"

4.   Yet, when the people did sip, the paper straw began to dissolve, leaving their drinks untouched. And they cried, "Why dost thou crumble, O Paper Straw? We have given thee our faith!"

5.   But the faithful, undeterred, declared, "It is but a small price to pay! The turtles shall be saved, and we shall be righteous!"

6.   Yet, all around them, mountains of plastic, wrapped in convenience, continued to grow. And the people said, "Surely, we must consume, for how else can we live in ease?"

7.   And though they cast away plastic packaging and bottles, they clung to the paper straw, as though it alone could mend the world.

8.   One spake, "What of all the waste that doth surround us? The straws are but a drop in the sea of waste!"

9.   And the wise one replied, "The paper straw, noble as it may seem, is but a token, while the rest of thy ways remain untouched. The waste doth overflow, and the straw crumbles before thy lips."

10.   Yet the people, blinded by virtue, continued to sip from their paper straws, their faces alight with pride, declaring, "We have done our part!"

11.   And one among them asked, "What good is a paper straw if the cup it fills be made of plastic?"

12.   But the faithful answered, "The straw is the first step! We have made our stand, and the turtles shall thank us!"

13.   And so the people continued, sipping their paper straws, oblivious to the mountains of waste all around them, saying, "The turtles are saved. The oceans are healed. What more is left?"

The Division of the Peasants 1–15

1.   And it came to pass that in the land of the Free, where once the people had striven for unity, there arose a new decree, called DEI—Diversity, Equity, and Inclusion.

2.   And the leaders spake, saying, "Let us divide the people according to their race, their gender, and their very being, that we may set the righteous apart from the wicked."

3.   And they proclaimed, "In the division of the people shall we find our virtue, and by separating the tribes, we shall heal the wounds of yore."

4.   And the people did ask, "But hath not the great civil war been fought? Hath not the land been made one by the blood of the fallen? How then shall we return to the days of division?"

5.   And the Wokies among them answered, saying, "Ye are blind! The work of old is undone. Let us divide, for only in separation shall we find salvation. The oppressed are the

righteous, and their wounds make them holy."

6. And behold, the more one suffered, the higher was their place in the land. The Wokies did declare, "We are righteous, for we wear the mantle of victimhood, and in our false suffering, we find our merit."

7. And the leaders spake, saying, "Let him who is most oppressed rise above all others. For the greater thy self-perceived oppression, the more he shall draweth unearned riches.

8. And they cast out those who spake against their ways, calling them heretics, bigots, and racists. And the people trembled, for to speak against them was to be cast into darkness.

9. And lo the elder, Joseph, the chosen ruler, spake unto the people, saying, "I shall appoint the one who is most virtuous among you, the one who is oppressed, for she shall lead the land based not on merit."

10. And he appointed the Cackler, saying, "Behold, she is a woman and she is brown in color, and thus she is worthy to lead. Her perceived suffering makes her pure, and in her, the land shall find its salvation."

11. And the Wokies did marvel, and they cheered, for they saw in the Cacklers rise the triumph of self-victimhood. They spake among themselves, "She is our chosen one. In her lack of merit, we see our own rise!"

12. And the land was divided, and the people were separated into tribes and factions, each claiming the high ground of righteousness, each declaring their own victimhood as the mark of their holiness.

13. And the DEI folk did build their temples, where only those who embraced separation could enter. And they spake, saying, "The righteous are those who

suffer the most, for their wounds make them pure."

14.   And the land became a land of division, where all who spake of unity were cast out and branded as oppressors, for to question the ways of DEI was to be uneducated, bigoted and blind to the truth.

15.   And lo, the Cackler sat upon her throne, and the Wokies continued to cheer, for they had embraced the virtue of self-victimhood, and in their separation, they believed they had found salvation.

Defunders of the Watchman 1–15

1.   And it came to pass that in the year of the Great Election, there arose a great noise in the land, a rumbling from the hearts of the people. The Orange Man, spake unto the multitudes, saying, "Let your voices be heard, but let them be peaceful."

2.   But behold, the enemies of the people, the Deep State, did speak in falsehoods, and they cried out, saying, "The Orange Man doth stir the hearts of the people to violence! He is the bringer of chaos, the instigator of rebellion!"

3.   And the multitudes did gather in the land's great Capitol, seeking to have their voices heard, but the authorities of the land, who wore the robes of deceit, said, "Let them be quiet, and let them be scattered."

4.   And lo, the Orange Man called out to

the people once more, "Be peaceful, be calm, and let not your hearts be filled with rage." But the enemies of peace, the Chamber of Echoes of falsehoods, spake louder still, crying, "The Orange Man hath incited an insurrection! He seeks to overthrow the land!"

5.   But verily, it was the Deep State and the uni-party who spread their lies, for they were the true enemies of the people, clothed in righteousness, yet filled with deceit.

6.   And behold, as the people of the Orange Man were falsely accused of insurrection, a great destruction did take place in the cities, for there arose the Defunders of the Watchmen, who were supported by none other than the Cackler herself!

7.   And they did burn and loot the cities, while they called it "love," and they called it "justice." They raised their banners and cried, "Defund the

Watchmen, for the system is racist!"

8.   And lo, in the city of the Giant Space Needle, they spake unto the people, saying, "We declare this land our own. This is CHAZ, this is CHOP. Here, we are free, and no man shall govern us!"

9.   And the Cackler, the face of D.E.I., and the elder, Joseph, the frail leader, spake not a word against the chaos. They did not rebuke the Defunders nor those who tore the land asunder. Nay, they cheered them on, saying, "This is the people's will, this is the land's righteousness!"

10.   But the Orange Man, whose heart was peaceful, did condemn the violence. He spake, "Let there be no violence, no destruction. Let the people speak, but let them not burn the cities nor cause harm!"

11.   And the people of the land did see this, but the enemies of the people did not hear. For they

declared the Orange Man the enemy, and they called him a threat to Democracy and an instigator of an insurrection.

12. And thus, they did lie, and they spread falsehoods, and they spake in the courts, saying, "The Orange Man sought to overthrow the people, to destroy the election, to cast down all that was good!"

13. But behold, the Defunders and the rioters were not rebuked. The Cackler and Joseph spake not a word against them, for their voices were their truth, and their destruction was their virtue.

14. And the people were confused, for they knew in their hearts that the true insurrection was not from the Orange Man, but from those who sought to divide, to destroy, and to tear the land asunder. Yet the leaders of the land did cheer, and they called it "the Days of Love," as they sowed division among the people.

15. And the people did cry out, saying, "When shall the truth be known? When shall justice be done? For the land has been divided, and the righteousness of peace has been cast out in favor of the deceit of power wielded by the Cackler and Joseph."

The Mysterious Powder
1-8

1.   And it came to pass, in the land of the White House, under the rule of Joseph and the Cackler, that a great mystery was afoot. For lo, a strange substance was discovered in the halls of power, white and powdery, hidden where the leaders dwell.

2.   The people were confused, for they knew not from whence this powder had come. The scent was unmistakable—like the winds of mischief and chaos. It was none other than the substance known as "pixie dust."

3.   And the Chamber of Echoes, with its many scribes, declared, "This is an enigma! Who among us would leave such a thing in the people's house? Surely, no noble soul would indulge in such a manner."

4.   And Joseph, with eyes wide and frail, looked upon the whimsical pixie dust and said, "I know not of this. I am but a servant of the people, and this powder is foreign to me."

5.   And the Cackler, ever ready to laugh, did cackle and declare, "This is simply a misunderstanding. Surely, no one here would dare to

partake in such things. Perhaps it was simply misplaced."

6.   But the people, knowing the ways of the land, whispered, "Whose whimsical pixie dust is this? Is it Joseph's? Is it the Cackler's? Or is it someone else's in the court?"

7.   And the Cackler, with a grin upon her face, did speak again, "This is no matter for the people. Let us simply blame it on the servants of the house and move on. Who would question the wisdom of the administration?"

8.   And so, the people waited, yet no answer came from the top. For the whimsical pixie dust, as quickly as it appeared, was forgotten in the whispers of the night.

The Mask of Tyranny 1-14

1.   And it came to pass that Joseph, the one who sat upon the throne of power, did decree that the people must cover their faces with masks, and that they must accept the needle of the plague, or they shall be shunned.

2.   "Let no one be free," said Joseph, "for the people must do as I command, and the Cackler, she did cheer, for her voice was full of power and control.

Together, they ruled with iron fists and a smile of false concern."

3.   But lo, the people did question. "Is it not the same Joseph who, with the Cackler, once called the Orange Man a tyrant, a dictator who sought to control the lives of the people?"

4.   Yet Joseph and the Cackler, in their new reign, did bind the people with orders that denied their freedom, and the mandates fell like chains upon their wrists.

5.　　And the people cried, "Is this not hypocrisy? Did not Joseph and the Cackler call the Orange Man a tyrant, yet they now wear the same crown of oppression? Did they not speak of liberty, only to chain us to their will?"

6.　　And lo, it was the highest court in the land, SCOTUS, that rose up and declared, "These mandates are unconstitutional! These orders are the tyranny you once condemned!"

7.　　"Oh, the hypocrisy," cried the people, for they had been deceived. "The very ones who railed against oppression now bring forth the same chains. The Cackler and Joseph are no better than the tyrants they once opposed."

8.　　And the judges, in their wisdom, did strike down the orders. "For the people shall not be ruled by fear," they said. "The law of the land is the law of liberty."

9.　　And Joseph, the once-praised leader, did stand humbled, for his power was stripped from him by the very court he had once respected. "This is not tyranny," he said, but the people knew better.

10.　　"Oh, how the mighty have fallen," said the Orange Man, who had once been labeled a tyrant. "For now it is Joseph and the Cackler who bear the mantle of hypocrisy."

11.　　And the people, though they had been deceived, did now see clearly. "The ones who spoke of freedom are now the ones who sought to take it from us," they whispered.

12.　　"Tyranny is a mask," they said, "and Joseph and the Cackler wore it well, yet they were unmasked by the wisdom of the court."

13.　　And so, it was that Joseph and the Cackler, whose masks were not of cloth but of power, did find themselves stripped

bare before the people,
for their hypocrisy could
not stand.
14.   And the people,
free once more, did
rejoice, for they knew
that true power lies not in
the hands of tyrants, but
in the hands of the
people.

The Reckoning

The Great Debate 1-15

1.   And lo, it came to pass in the land of America that Joseph, former second-hand man to the first well-spoken black leader, was heralded as a man of wit and vigor, sharp as an arrow and swift in tongue as proclaimed by the Chamber of Echoes.

2.   Yet, whispers among the people said, "But is not Joseph aged as the ancient cedars? Does his mind not wander as the lost sheep?" But, the Chambers of Echoes, also known as, Mainstreamia, heeded not these murmurings, for their trust was firmly placed in their championed marionette of the Deep State.

3.   And so it was that a great debate was called

upon, where Joseph would stand against the Orange Man, known across the lands for his boisterous proclamations and the art of the tweet.

4.   When the debate began, Joseph stood with his back straight, his suit immaculate, yet his eyes were wide and distant, as if he had just awakened in a strange land and did not know the road that led him there. He stared ahead, seemingly lost, and for a moment, it was as if time itself had paused around him.

5.   Joseph opened his mouth, and from it came not the eloquence promised, but a river of wandering thoughts. "Behold! We hath finally beateth Medicare."

6.   To which the Orange Man replied, "Thou hast beateth it to death". Joseph, undeterred, gazed into the distance and spoke once more, " We must—uh—come on, man!"

7.   The Orange Man, ever quick with his tongue and his wit, raised a brow, looked at the biased moderators, and declared, "I know not what he spake at the end thereof, and verily, I deem he knoweth not either!"

8.   Joseph's handlers, seated among the Socialites of America, cringed in their silken robes. They whispered among themselves, "Did he not practice with the scrolls and rehearse the proverbs of the Deep State?"

9.   Yet, despite the fumbling, the scribes quickly inked their parchments and sent forth their scrolls, declaring, "Joseph did mightily in the battle of words, valiantly holding his ground, even when his words meandered like the rivers of Babbleon."

10.   But among the common folk, tales were spun of the night Joseph spoke of Medicare. "Did he not say it himself?" they jested in the markets and taverns. "The man

who bested healthcare with but one breath."

11. After the debate, the rulers of America came nigh unto Joseph and said unto him, "Joseph, wilt thou now step down, for the defeat was great, and the people witnessed it?"

12. And Joseph, with a weary smile, declared, "I shall back down only if God himself descends from the heavens and commands me so."

13. And lo, the heavens remained silent, with not a divine whisper or heavenly light to be seen. Yet, in time, Joseph stepped aside, proclaiming, "I send my blessings to the Cackler, who shall now carry forth the banner against the Orange Man."

14. Thus, the Cackler was chosen to replace him in the race, and America rejoiced, though some still whispered, "Did not Joseph say he would only step down by divine decree?" But none dared question further.

15. And so ended the tale of the great debate, where Joseph's sharpness was tested and found wanting, and the people pondered the path that lay ahead.

Cackler of Joy 1-15

1.   And lo, on the sixty sixth day of the sixth cycle, as God surveyed His creation, He thought, "This is all pretty good, but something's missing… something meek, mild, and utterly incapable of taking initiative."

2.   And He spoke, saying, "Let there be Betas, the White Duds, who shall walk this earth in reverence, their eyes ever fixed upon the mighty Cackler."

3.   And so, the Lord fashioned the Betas from the dullest, most unassertive dust, with their backs hunched and their eyes downcast. They were designed not to lead, but to nod. To agree. To laugh nervously at every chuckle the Cackler unleashed.

4.   "Behold," said the Lord, "These Betas shall not know the sound of their own voices. Their

lives shall consist of responding 'yass queen' to every inspirational quote the Cackler shares, and they shall laugh whenever she cackles, even when they don't understand why."

5.   And He placed them in the Land of Suburbia, where they could endlessly debate who had the best quinoa salad recipe, while the Cacklers cackles echoed in the background, like the laugh of a distant, benevolent overlord.

6.   "The Cackler shall bring joy," the Lord proclaimed, "A joy that is radiant, ever-present, and unmistakably hollow. And the Betas, delusional in their devotion, shall eat it up like manna from the heavens."

7.   And the Cacklers joy came not in the form of profound wisdom or mighty acts, but in a stream of hearty, entirely unnerving cackles that seemed to emerge at the most unexpected moments—at speeches, at questions, even at moments of sheer silence.

8.   "She spreads this joy," the Lord said, "not to enlighten, but to enchant. And enchanted they shall be, these Betas, for they shall see her laughter as a beacon of hope, even if it sounds like an inside joke they will never be in on."

9.   And the Betas, full of false joy and trepidation, nodded solemnly, saying, "Her cackle is a divine signal! When she laughs, it is as if the pits of hell themselves crack open and all morons are revealed. Truly, only she can save democracy."

10.   "Now go, my Betas," said the Lord, "Help the Cackler win the Election for the Woke People. For through this great and glorious election, you shall save Democracy itself."

11.   And so the Betas, the White Duds, set forth on their quest, armed only with their smartphones, their unshakable faith in

the Cacklers greatness, and a bumper stickers on their Prius' that read "Joy to all of those who agree with us; Stoned to death shall be those whom do not."

12.　They knocked on doors (but only when it was convenient), handed out flyers (but only to people who already agreed with them), and typed furiously on social media, pushing their "We're Not Going Back" campaign with the fervor of a millennial trying to secure a spot on an influencer's Podcast.

13.　And whenever she cackled, they would throw their heads back in forced joy, for it was said that her laughter was a cure for all things sane. "This is true happiness," they whispered to themselves, ignoring the strange hollowness it left behind.

14.　"The Cackler must win," they said, "For if she does not, Democracy will collapse like a poorly made vegan souffle."

15.　And the Betas laughed on command, like trained seals, every time she cackled. The more her laugh echoed, the more the Betas saw it as a sign of her cosmic greatness. They laughed, too—out of nervousness, yes, but mostly because they were supposed to.

Endorsements 1-15

1.   And it came to pass that the Cackler, who spoke with laughter like a thousand deranged crows, did raise her voice for the Wokies.

2.   And lo, the White Duds and the Betas did gather in support, shouting praises of her joy, though it was a joy that none could trust.

3.   Yet among the loudest voices of praise were the Cheneys, the mighty family of war and profit, the ones who had spilled much blood upon the earth.

4.   For they had walked the paths of war with Halliburton, their temple of industry, and did trade in the riches of conflict, yea, even as the people wept for peace.

5.   And the followers of the Cackler did rejoice greatly, for they believed that the Cheneys' blessing was a sign of peace, a sign that the Cackler was the bearer of great power.

6.   "Surely, peace is upon us," they cried, "for the Cheneys, with all their might, have chosen the Cackler as their champion."

7.   But the followers of the Orange Man, they who had eyes to see and ears to hear, did not rejoice. For they knew that the ways of the Cheneys were the ways of war, not of peace.

8.   And they did speak unto the people, saying, "Behold, the endorsement of the warmongers is not a sign of peace, but of the Deep State's eternal grip upon this land."

9.   For the Cheneys, in all their glory, did once send the children of the land to fight in distant wars, and filled their coffers with gold from the deaths of others.

10.   And they who followed the Orange Man did declare, "This is not a sign of power, but a sign of the false powers that still pull the strings behind the throne."

11.   Thus the Deep State, with its marionettes of war and money, remained strong, and the people knew that the Cackler's ascent was not to end the wars but to continue the cycle.

12.   And the Cackler, hearing the voices of both praise and doubt, did continue to laugh, for she knew not the weight of the strings she pulled.

13.   But lo, the doubters did cry out in the land, "This is not the way of peace. This is the way of the puppeteers, and they laugh while the world burns."

14.   And the people, confused, did wonder whether the warmongers' blessing was a curse, for in their hearts they knew that peace cannot come from those who have fed upon war.

15.   And so it was that the Deep State, with its endless wars and endless power, did remain ever the shadow upon the land, even as the Cackler stood in the light, laughing and leading.

The Chamber of Echoes

1.   And lo, the Chamber of Echoes raised its voice, louder than before, crying out to the people: "Beware, O ye gullible souls, for Project 2025 threatens to destroy the very ones we seek to protect!"

2.   They cried, "This is no mere plan, but a shadow of the Orange Man that stretches across all, and it shall bring oppression, division, and the undoing of all that the Wokies have fought for!"

3.   And the Wokies, asked, "What is this Project 2025, and where does its power lie?" The Chamber spake in fear mongering tongues, weaving riddles and falsehoods that their victims could not untangle

4. Alongside these warnings, the Chamber declared, "Fear the MAGA who reject the echoes of Mainstreamia and deny those with testicles who choose to identify as women, and hath wary thoughts of the zay-zims—these are the ones who bring forth the Project 2025 agenda!"

5. And the Chamber swore, "Trust us, for only we can save you! Only through us can you understand the grave danger that lies in Project 2025—this movement to silence and oppress the zay-zims, the men who 'become' women, and all the enlightened ones who challenge the status quo!"

6. But the wise among the people scoffed, saying, "Is not this Project 2025 a shadow fabricated by the Chamber itself, a tool to control and manipulate by instilling fear?"

7. Yet the Chamber pressed on, repeating its mantra: "If you do not stand against Project 2025, you are complicit in its fascism. If you do not fight for the zay-zims and the men who wish to bear children, you are enemies of love and progress."

8. And the wokies, eager to champion what they believed was a righteous cause, took up the banner of the Chamber, repeating its cries and calling for action against the supposed threat of Project 2025.

9. But others said, "We do not fear Project 2025, for we see it as nothing more than a phantom. The real threat is the Chamber itself, spreading fear where there is none, manipulating the vulnerable with their deceitful tongues."

10. The wise laughed at the absurdity that men could bear children or transform into women, saying, "Can a stone bear fruit, or a river turn to fire? These are not truths but twisted fables meant

to control and confound."

11.   Yet the wokies, blinded by their beliefs, branded these voices "uneducated" and "bigoted," for the Magafolk refused to accept the illusion the Chamber had created.

12.   The Chamber's voice grew louder still, repeating its warnings: "Do not doubt us! Project 2025 will destroy all that is good, and the men who pretend to be women, and the zay-zims, shall be cast into darkness!"

13.   But as the truth began to emerge, the people saw that the Chamber was built not on truth, but on manipulation, a machine to spread fear and keep them divided.

14.   They said, "Let the zay-zims live as they choose, and let men who identify as women be who they wish. They hold no power over us except that which we grant them. Their struggles are theirs, not some tool of destruction."

15.   The people laughed at the falsehoods, saying, "Shall a man bear a child, or a woman become a man with a mere thought? These are fantasies, not reality!"

16.   And as the Chamber of Echoes grew ever more desperate, its cries were met with indifference, for the people saw through the deceit, and the fear it had sown began to fade.

17.   They declared, "No longer will we live by fear, nor will we be manipulated by those who profit from our anxieties. We will no longer listen to the empty echoes of the Chamber, for we know it is built on lies."

18.   And so the Chamber faltered, for its strength lay not in truth, but in the hearts and minds it had once ensnared. Without their belief, its power crumbled, and the people found their freedom again.

19.   They said,

"Project 2025 was but a shadow, a creation of fear, meant to divide us. It had no true power except that which the Chamber fed into it." 20. And thus, the Chamber of Echoes was silenced, its grip broken, for the people had seen the truth—the only thing to fear was the fear itself, and the lies that had held them captive

The Great Fellowship

Man of the Stars 1-16

1.   Elon, Man of the Stars, came from a faraway land, a man of rockets and cosmic dreams. His heart burned with the desire to restore the First Pillar—free speech—to the people. The town square, known to the people as Twitter, had fallen into the hands of the Chamber of Echoes and the Deep State.

2.   These dark forces sought to silence the voices of the people, and the First Pillar was crumbling. The town square had become a battleground for words, but the people's voices were drowned out by the elite.

3.   And Elon, full of resolve, said, "I shall purchase the town square and free thy people's tongues. No longer shall the Deep State control the speech of the land."

4.   So, with great vision, Elon took up his coin and purchased the town square. And to symbolize his victory, he threw in the kitchen sink, declaring, "I shall give it all to restore your voices. The town square is once again free."

5.   And the people cheered, for they believed their freedom had been restored. The town square was once again theirs to speak in.

6.   But as Elon walked deeper into the town square, he uncovered a great secret hidden beneath the surface. For within the vaults of Twitter lay the ancient laptop of Hunter, Joseph's son.

7.   And Elon, with great curiosity, sought the truth of the laptop. But lo, he discovered that 51 Deep State agents had conspired to hide the laptop, calling it "Russian misinformation," lest the people learn its secrets.

8.   And Elon, undeterred, called forth the scribes to reveal the Twitter Scrolls. The truth was clear—it held evidence of corruption and misdeeds hidden from the people, and the Deep State had worked to keep it buried.

9.   "Why was this truth hidden?" Elon asked. "Why was the laptop falsely labeled and kept from the people? I have come to restore the truth, not to bury it."

10.   And the people, hearing this, marveled. For they had been deceived, and now the truth was before them. The Deep State had hidden the truth to maintain control, but Elon had brought it into the light.

11.   But the Chamber of Echoes, ever fearful of losing its hold on power, said, "This man is the bringer of misinformation. He is not the savior, but the destroyer."

12.   And the people, confused by the words of the Chamber of Echoes,

began to murmur. "But he has restored the town square! He has freed our voices! How is he the bringer of lies?"

13. Yet, the Deep State pressed on, and Elon, though he had restored free speech, was labeled the enemy. They said, "He is the spreader of chaos. He must be stopped."

14. And so, Elon stood tall, saying, "I came to give the people their voices. If they wish to speak, they shall. The truth is theirs to decide."

15. And still, the Chamber of Echoes called him the enemy, the villain, the one who brought forth misinformation. But Elon knew that he had done what was right.

16. The town square had been reclaimed, but the struggle for truth and speech was far from over. The people, now free to speak, would fight to keep their voices from being silenced again.

The Questioner 1-20

1. And it came to pass that in the land of Modernia, there arose a great and peculiar plague known as COVID, which swept across the nations, causing the people to hoard toilet paper, Zoom endlessly, and fashion masks from old underpants.

2. And in these days, the people cried out for a savior, for their leaders offered them daily updates that left them none the wiser and the confusion spread faster than the plague itself.

3. From the House of Kennedy, there emerged one named Robby, known by some as RFK, and by others as "The Black Sheep of Questions." And he bore a message unto the people: "Let us question what we are told, for not every needle brings salvation."

4. And lo, the people were divided. Some cried, "Yea, this man is a truth-sayer, for Big Pharma

holds much gold and wields much influence!" While others, scrolling Twitter with furrowed brows, whispered, "Nay, this man is anti-vax, a heretic to science!"

5.   But RFK stood tall, saying, "I am not against all potions, only those brewed with haste, whose makers share a goblet with Greed." And he spake of the days of yore when potions were tested through many moons before they were declared safe.

6.   And from the highest towers of Modernia's media, voices rang out: "Beware! He who questions the potion spreads misinformation!" And they clanged their symbols and flashed their banners with alarming headlines, most of which were crafted in haste and shared with fervor.

7.   And there in the shadow of this uproar stood a man named Fauci, Chief of Needles and Lord of Lockdowns. With each briefing, he spake

unto the people, and each time his words would twist and turn as serpents do in the desert.

8.   "Trust in the Science," said Fauci, though it changed its mind more often than a wokies gender. "Take thy potions, one, two, then three, and even four! Blessed are those who receive the booster, for they shall dine at the restaurants of Modernia once more."

9.   And the people of Modernia obeyed, for fear was greater than inquiry, and Fauci's words were carried on scrolls from the Chamber of Echoes. Yet some, who dared think for themselves, whispered of side effects and sudden silence among those who questioned too loudly.

10.   Among these whispers, the name Rogan was heard, a man of podcasts and mighty questions. And it came to pass that he, stricken with COVID, took a remedy

known to horse and man alike: Ivermectin.

11. "Behold!" cried the keepers of headlines, "He consumes the horse dewormer, unfit for man!" And they smirked and guffawed in the town square of Twitter and all across the Chamber of Echoes, declaring him a fool, though behind closed doors, the potion was known for more than just equine cure.

12. RFK beheld this madness and spake, "Why mock those who seek health through means not bought by gold? Hath not the world once laughed at ideas before they were embraced? Woe to those who forget the lessons of history for the sake of trending hashtags."

13. And Fauci, feeling the whispers rise, summoned his ally, Bill of the Great Socialites, who appeared in documentaries and panels, expounding on needles. And together they funded great campaigns, where potions were blessed and questions were cursed.

14. Yet RFK stood undeterred, declaring, "I come not to end Science but to cleanse it of its gilded chains." And some, hearing this, began to murmur, "Make America Healthy Again!" and they wore shirts bearing this slogan, though cautiously, lest the scorn of the media rain down upon them.

15. And the great Chamber of Echoes continued their dance, mocking and jesting at the non-compliers, while praising those who boosted thrice and wore double masks, even when alone in their chariots.

16. And thus it was that Modernia remained split. Some embraced every jab with the zeal of the faithful, posting their proofs of potion-taking as badges of honor. Others watched, wary and skeptical, sharing memes in secret and speaking in code.

17. But in the end, RFK gathered his followers and said, "Let us not be swayed by shouts from the towers, but seek truth as it is, plain and unmasked." And his voice, though mocked by many, reached the ears of those who still dared question.

18. And it was written: In Modernia, where the Cackler cackled, the Lord of Lockdowns ruled, and the scrolls of the Deep State scribes fluttered in the wind, the quest for truth persisted, for in the heart of man, the desire for freedom is stronger than the fear of disapproval.

19. And the people of common sense, hidden among the multitude, nodded quietly, knowing they had seen this tale before. And they waited, watching, for the day when questions would no longer be silenced, and the noise of false prophets would be drowned out by clarity.

20. And so it was, and so it shall be. Amen.

The Warrior of Peace 1-15

1.   And it came to pass that the great debate of words was held in the land where leaders gathered to display their cunning and win the favor of the people. And there, among the many voices that clamored for attention, stood Tulsi, the Warrior of Peace, and the Cackler, whose laughter resounded like bleats from goats.

2.   The Cackler, adorned in robes of ambition, smiled her knowing smile, for she believed her place among the leaders was secure. Her past, shrouded in tales of power and verdicts, was hidden by the noise of her laugh.

3.   But Tulsi, seeing the people confused by the mirth that masked misdeeds, stepped forward and raised her voice, saying, "O people, ye have heard the tales spun by the Cackler, who boasts of justice and order. But I ask, whose justice? And at what price?"

4.   The Cackler's smile faltered as she glared like a stool pigeon

caught in a web of deceit. She let out a cackle, sharp and sudden, to drown out the whispers. But Tulsi's voice was steady as the sea. "Let us not forget," said the Warrior, "the days when the Cackler sat high in the land of Golden Dominion, wielding the gavel as a scepter."

5.   And the crowd stirred, for these words were bold, and the air grew tense. Tulsi continued, "Yea, she who claims to fight for the downtrodden, did she not once lock away those who were poor and desperate? Did she not, with the swiftness of the gavel, seal the fate of those who were innocent, even when their pleas echoed through the halls?"

6.   The Cackler's laughter turned brittle, and her hands clenched as if to grasp the invisible threads of her defense. But no mirth could shield her now, for the truth had been spoken aloud.

7.   "And what of the scrolls of evidence?" Tulsi pressed, her eyes unwavering. "Did not the Cackler keep them sealed, even when justice called out for their unveiling? Yea, let the people know that beneath the laughter lies a tale of power pursued at any cost."

8.   The crowd gasped, and even the scribes of the Chamber of Echoes, who scribbled furiously, could not erase what they had heard.

9.   The Warriors gaze sharpened, and she said, "Ask her of the days when she was questioned if she had ever partaken of the herb that grows wild. Yea, when asked if she had ever smoked the weed for which so many were imprisoned under her rule, did she not laugh? A laugh that mocked the very souls she had condemned?"

10.   And the crowd, remembering this, muttered among themselves, for the laughter that once

charmed now rang hollow, a reminder of justice denied and truth obscured.

11.   And the Cackler, seeing that her laughter could no longer silence the truth, stood motionless, her eyes darting like those of a cornered beast. Yet no word, nor chuckle, escaped her lips, for the Warriors words had chained them.

12.   And the scribes of the Chamber of Echoes, loyal to the Cackler and her ways, were wroth, for they favored her delighted in her laugh. "How dare this Warrior speak against the chosen one!" they cried, their quills scribbling furiously. "She is no Warrior of honor; behold, she is but a spy of Russia!"

13.   And so they wrote upon their parchments, their voices echoing from the glowing boxes,

"Tulsi, the brave, is not of us; she is of the foreign lands, an agent sent to sow discord!" And the people, confused by the many voices of America, pondered in doubt.

14.   But even with their tales and slanders, the truth of Tulsi's words stood firm. And though branded falsely as a spy, the Warrior was victorious, for she had unmasked the Cackler and shown the people that laughter could hide much, but not everything.

15.   And so it was that the Cackler, though favored by the Chamber of Echoes, was bested in that battle, and the tale of the Warrior's triumph was told. And the people of common sense said among themselves, "The spy, they called her, but truth and wisdom was the power of the Warrior of Peace."

The Man of Merit 1-10

1.   And lo, from the land of the rising tech moguls, there came forth a man known as Vivek, a son of the digital age. He was not born into the traditions of the elders, but was instead molded by algorithms and the mighty power of investment.

2.   And it came to pass that Vivek, seeing the state of the land, did rise with a new vision, a vision unlike any seen before. He proclaimed unto the people, "I will free you from the shackles of mediocrity, for I have seen the light of entrepreneurial spirit!"

3.   And the people looked upon him and were puzzled, for they knew not what this light was, nor how one could be freed from mediocrity by talking about the wonders of capitalism in all its glory. But Vivek spoke with confidence, and his words sparkled like gold coins in the sun.

4.   He did proclaim, "The system is broken, and I, Vivek, shall fix it! The government is bloated, and the media is a snake pit. Only through innovation and the spirit of competition can we truly reach greatness!"

5.   And lo, Vivek spake against the great idols of DEI—those that worshiped the holy trinity of diversity, equity, and inclusion. He declared, "Hiring by skin, gender,

or identity is but a farce. Let the people be judged by their skills and merit, not the color of their skin or the shape of their names!"

6.   And the people, hearing this new doctrine, did nod their heads. "Finally," they said, "someone who values the sweat of the brow and the fire of the mind, not the labels placed upon us by others!"

7.   But the Chamber of Echoes , seeing this man with no long history in the halls of power, did scoff. They called him a newcomer, a disruptor without cause, and said, "He is but a man of wealth and ambition, not of wisdom or tradition!"

8.   But Vivek, undeterred, spake, "I am neither a politician nor a pawn. I am the future, and the future cannot be bound by the chains of the past. My ideas are free, and my path is clear. Follow me into the New Age!"

9.   And lo, as he spoke, the people rallied behind him, for they had grown tired of being shackled by the idea that merit should take a backseat to identity. "Let the best ideas and the hardest workers rise!" they declared.

10.   And though the doubters and critics were many, the people who longed for a change, a break from the old ways, began to gather in numbers. They knew not what the future held, but they believed, at the very least, it would be different. And thus, Vivek marched forth, a man unafraid to challenge the established powers, with a plan that none had yet seen but all were eager to imagine.

The Weird One and His Mamaw 1-15

1.   And it came to pass in the days of the Orange Man, who spoke in the tongue of tweets and roused the multitudes with the fervor of his proclamations, that he sought a companion, one with the fire of wit and the strength to confound the scribes of Chamber of Echoes.

2.   And lo, there appeared James David of the Vance, from the rugged hills of Middletown, clad not in golden robes but in the garments of one who had walked among the common folk and knew their trials. For he was no stranger to struggle, having been raised in the shadow of hardship and the love of a fierce matriarch known to all as Mamaw.

3.   Now, Mamaw was a woman of iron resolve and a tongue that loosed words sharper than any blade. Mamaw's words of wisdom and love were peppered with curses that rolled from her lips like thunder. And J.D., her grandson, held her lessons close, learning to speak with boldness even when others faltered.

4.   The Orange Man beheld him and said, "Thou art strange, for thou speakest with wisdom, yet the Chamber of Echoes cannot fathom thee. Thou shalt be my chosen sidekick, for they call thee 'weird,' but I call thee a warrior of words."

5.   J.D. of the Vance had chronicled his journey in the scroll known as Hillbilly Elegy, wherein he spoke of his mother, who wrestled with the chains of addiction, and the many souls trapped in the clutches of despair in towns where hope was as scarce as gold. The people saw in him a reflection of their own tales, yet the scribes of the Echoes found no favor in his words.

6.   And so it was that the Weird One stood by the side of the Orange Man, and the scribes of Echoes were sorely vexed. They gathered in their towers, muttering, "Who is this man that twists our tales and laughs at our lamentations? He speaks as if born of the people, yet he dares defy us with his cunning!"

7.   They cried, "He is not like us; behold, he is peculiar, a spectacle! Let it be written that he is odd, that he is strange, that he is to be feared for his weirdness!" And they sent forth their heralds to declare, "J.D. Vance is not one of us! Hear, O people, he is… weird!"

8.   But the Weird One., the chosen of the Orange Man, knew the ways of the scribes. He took their words, turned them in his grasp like a craftsman shaping clay, and sent them back with such force that the towers of the Deep State trembled.

9.   "Thou callest me 'weird,'" he said, "yet it is thy words that dance upon falsehoods and twist like serpents. I am not bound by thy scripts, nor do I seek favor from thy ink-stained quills. For I

come not from the gilded halls but from homes where hunger and hope wage battle, where voices like Mamaw's thunder and mothers seek redemption."

10.   And the people, who once doubted, began to see. For J.D. the Weird One spoke with the voice of those who had been forgotten, who knew the weight of despair but also the fire of resilience.

11.   The scribes of Echoes, red-faced and confounded, could not silence him nor make him fit their tales. They clutched their parchments and proclaimed, "He is not one of us! He cannot be trusted, for he wears his past like a badge and defies our judgment. He had the audacity to jest upon the women of the feline order"

12.   But J.D., who had faced greater storms than the quills of scribes, turned their judgments into laughter that echoed across the land. And those who sought to shame him found themselves shamed, for he turned their accusations into proof of their own shallowness.

13.   The Orange Man, seeing this, roared with approval, saying, "Behold, my sidekick, who has made the mockers fall silent and the wise look foolish."

14.   And so it was that J.D. of the Vance, the so-called 'Weird' One, became a thorn in the sides of the Chamber of Echoes, who whispered and wailed but could not prevail. The people who watched from afar said, "Truly, he is one of us, for he knows the song of hardship and the dance of triumph."

15.   And thus the tale of the Weird One spread across the land, from the great towers of the Deep State to the smallest homes. And the people saw that to be called 'weird' by those who twist the truth is, perhaps, a mark of honor.

The Deliverance of Greatness

Crimson Tide 1-24

1.   And lo, upon the far horizon, there arose a mighty deliverance—a storm of crimson and flame, the Gigantic Red Wave, sweeping across the land with a fury none could deny. The Orange Man, in his glory, did declare, "Behold, this is the greatest wave the world hath ever seen—greater than the seas of old, greater than any wave before it, greater than any wave that shall come!"

2.   And the Voice of the People, united with the Orange Man, did strike the Wokies and the Betas like a fierce, untamed tweet in the darkest hours of night. It was a sound that shook the very heavens, a noise brash and bold, full of might and power. It was a sound that echoed across the land, shaking the hearts of the Betas, who

had never known such boldness.

3.　　The Wokies and the Betas, weak and trembling, gathered in their sanctuaries—with their Wi-Fi routers—and cried out in desperation, "O Cackler, come forth! Tweet once more to save us from this Red Wave!" But alas, the Cackler did not answer. There was silence, and the Betas were left with naught but their trembling hands.

4.　　And the Lord, watching from His throne, spake unto the Wokies and the Betas, saying, "The battle is done. The Wokies and the Betas have fallen, for they were too passive. Yet, in their passivity, they bore a bitter intolerance, and their voice was as faint as a 'subtweet' unnoticed by the masses. Lo, they have no power to turn back this tide."

5.　　And the Red Wave surged onward, relentless and unyielding, no force could halt its advance—not hashtags, nor dreams of a perfect Twitter thread. The Orange Man, like a great conqueror, did march forth, declaring unto the land, "We shall Make America Great Again!" His voice rang out with such vigor that the Wokies and Betas quivered before it.

6.　　The Wokies and Betas, in their last attempt to resist, tried to laugh in solidarity, but their chuckles were weak, uncertain, devoid of the Cackler's bold guffaw that could silence the heavens. "Perchance if we laugh louder, she will return," they murmured in their hearts, but their laughter was as hollow as their resolve.

7.　　And the Lord spake again, saying, "Ye cannot laugh your way out of this, O Wokies and Betas. Ye cannot meme your way into victory when the Red Wave, like a flood, doth engulf you. Go ye home, for the time of your reign is over."

8. And the Red Wave did continue, rising higher still, sweeping the land in its wake. No power could stay its course, and the Orange Man, with a fire in his eyes, did proclaim, "The people have spoken! The greatest wave in all of history hath come, and it shall carry this land to the freedom and greatness that once was!"

9. And the Wokies and Betas, defeated and broken, could do naught but watch as the Orange Man claimed his rightful place, restoring the land to its former glory. The White Duds, cried in their tweets and crushed beneath the weight of their own defeat, retreated into the shadows.

10. But lo, the Orange Man stood tall, a beacon of power and triumph, his hands raised high in victory. "I have returned!" he cried, "And with me, we shall restore the greatness that was lost. For I, and MAGA, are the bringers of the Red Wave, and no evil shall stand before it!"

11. And so it was, that the Wokies and Betas, whose dreams of saving Democracy through endless praise and retweets were dashed upon the rocks and were vanquished forever.

12. The Cackler, who once rode high upon her throne, had fallen silent, her influence shattered by the force of the Orange Man's return. The Wokies and Betas had no voice left to speak, no power to resist. "The Red Wave hath come, and the land is mine," declared the Orange Man, and MAGA cheered, for they knew their time had come.

13. And thus, it was written in the annals of history: "The Red Wave hath risen and shall never be overturned. The Orange Man, the greatest of Presidents, hath returned to stand for The People, even the Wokies and Betas."

14. But lo, the Orange Man and his loyal followers, the MAGA, had long been maligned, cast down by the powerful forces of the Chamber of Echoes and the Deep State, who had conspired to belittle and shame them. They were marked as fools, as the very bane of the land, accused of ignorance and hatred towards the brown skins.

15. And the Chamber of Echoes, with its eyes turned blind to justice, did mock the Orange Man, seeking to silence his voice, casting forth lies and deceit upon him. The Deep State, with its shadowy influence, sought to thwart his every move, casting falsehoods and devising wicked plots to bring him low.

16. Yet, despite the scorn and the treachery, the Orange Man did not falter. No, he arose once more, stronger and mightier, for he was not one to bend to the will of the wicked. His cause was just, and the people knew it. And the Red Wave did rise, sweeping all in its path, bringing justice to true patriots who had been oppressed for so long.

17. "Lo, we have been forsaken by the powers that be!" cried the Orange Man, as the Red Wave surged forth. "We hath been called haters, we hath been cast as enemies of the land. Yet here we stand, undaunted, and the time of our redemption hath come!"

18. And the land did rejoice, for the mighty wave had crushed the forces of oppression. Yet, in their defeat, the bitter ones—those of the Chamber of Echoes—did not turn to repentance. Nay, they grew bitter still, their anger twisted and directed at those they once held dear. "The Cackler hath fallen!" they cried, "The Orange Man hath defeated us! And now we turn upon those who hath betrayed us!"

19.   And lo, the Chamber of Echoes, now poisoned with pride and envy, turned upon their own, for the brown skins, those they had once championed, had risen in greater numbers to support the Orange Man, for they knew the truth. And so, the Chamber of Echoes, in their fury, cried out, "The brown skins are the enemies of progress, they are bigots, racists, and misogynists! They have betrayed us!"

20.   The very people whom the Chamber of Echoes had so long professed to protect, they now cast aside. And those of the brown skins, who had stood with the Orange Man and the Red Wave, did not waver. They knew who their true champion was, for the Orange Man had shown them that freedom and strength were not the purview of one color or another.

21.   And so it was that the Chamber of Echoes, in their defeat, turned against all who had once been their perceived allies. Their bitterness grew, and their fingers pointed everywhere but where the blame belonged. "It is not we who are to blame," they cried, "but those who have risen against us. It is their fault that the Cackler hath failed. It is their fault that the Red Wave hath triumphed!"

22.   Yet the truth remained: The Orange Man, with his mighty will and unwavering resolve, had reclaimed his place in the annals of history. And the Red Wave, a wave of justice and redemption, continued to rise. The Betas, the Wokies, the Cackler, and the Chamber of Echoes could do naught but watch as their reign came to an end. While everyone had forgotten Joseph.

23.   And it was declared across the land: "The Red Wave hath come, and with it, redemption for those who have been wronged. The

Orange Man is victorious, and his enemies, both foreign and domestic, shall know the weight of his triumph."

24.   And so it was written in the books of the ages: "The people hath spoken, and they shall be heard. The Cackler and her ilk have fallen, and the Red Wave shall reign supreme.

The Draining of the Swamp 1-10

1.   And lo, in the fullness of time, the Orange One, who had long declared, "Drain the swamp! Drain the swamp!" did gather unto himself a fellowship of five mighty souls. And with them, he set forth upon the great task of cleansing the land, for the swamp was rife with corruption, deceit, and untruths.

2.   First, there came the Weird One, whose wisdom and wit were unmatched. He stood as the second hand to the Orange One, wielding the sword of truth against the falsehoods of the Chamber of Echoes. And his voice, though laced with humor, struck fear in the hearts of those who hid in shadows, their lies and their deceit unraveling beneath his gaze.

3.   And with him, the Man of the Stars, who did

74

restore the First Pillar—the sacred freedom of speech, long hindered by the oppressors. The Man of the Stars proclaimed with great boldness, "Let all voices be heard, let none be silenced, for the truth shall shine like the stars in the heavens above!" And thus, the First Pillar was restored to its rightful place, a beacon for all to follow.

4.   Then there was the Man of Merit, who spoke of greatness not through birthright nor privilege, but through deeds and hard work. "I will hold the levers of power," he said, "with efficiency and justice, so that the people may prosper, for the swamp of bureaucracy must be drained." And so, he and the Man of the Stars, took the mantle of the Department of Government Efficiency, that they might smite the wasteful ways of the bureaucrats and prevent the squandering of gold on foolishness such as the making of mechanical squirrels, wrought to spy upon the serpents of the wilderness.

5.   And the Questioner, whose unyielding inquiries did unravel the lies of the false prophets, stood firm against the great beast known as Big Pharma. "Let the people be healed," he declared, "for the false prophets have made the people sick with their potions, and it is time for the healers to rise." And the Questioner set forth, bringing truth to power, casting aside the falsehoods of those who profited from the suffering of the people.6.

But lo, there came the Warrior, who spake of peace yet wielded the strength of a million mighty warriors. She took the mantle of National Intelligence, with a vision for peace that stretched across the world. "I shall not seek war," she said, "but I will protect the peace with the strength of a thousand warriors, for it is by peace we shall stand strong, united."

7.   And together, this Glorious Fellowship, led by the Orange One, set forth to drain the swamp. Their strength was in unity, their purpose clear. "We shall make America great once again," declared the Orange One, "and together, we shall rid this land of the corruption that has festered for too long."

8.   And thus, the swamp began to recede, for the forces of truth, merit, and justice had come to cleanse it. The people watched in awe as the fellowship wrought change upon the land, purging the swamp of its filth.9. Yet, there was great resistance, for the swamp fought back with all its might, summoning its minions of deceit and corruption. But the fellowship was undeterred, for they knew the battle was not just theirs, but that of the people. And the people cried out for freedom, for truth, and for justice.

10.   And so it was and so it shall be, that the swamp, though mighty, began to wither and shrink. The fellowship had proven stronger, and the land of America was restored to its rightful glory. And the Orange One, with his fellowship, had triumphed, for their victory was not just a victory over the swamp, but a victory for the people, for the truth, and for the freedom that would shine bright for generations to come.

God Hath Made America Great Once Again

The End

Made in the USA
Columbia, SC
23 November 2024

46899887R10043